Stand Out,

Fit In,

Get Hired:

Learn how to craft the perfect
resume for your dream job

By Brandon Trew

Contents

Red Laurie Press

Stand out, fit in, get hired: Learn how to craft the perfect resume for your dream role.
Brandon Trew

Copyeditor: FirstEditing.com
Interior and Cover Design: vook.com

Published in the United States by Red Laurie Press
ASIN: B00BGI49IE
ISBN-13: 978-1491208281
Version 2.0 (updated July 20th 2013)
Updates: http://standout-fitin-gethired.com

Blurbs

"[Brandon's] approach to crafting the perfect resume meshes well with what I have been writing about here at Quality Resumes for the past three years…. This is a book that will push and challenge you to create a powerful sales pitch. After all, that is what applying for a job is really all about—selling yourself to potential employers."

—Steve Brady, quality-resumes.com

"Having managed thousands of candidates vying for jobs at Google, I can easily say this book will make anyone a recruiter's dream. The author succinctly tackles each key part of the application process and addresses (with perfect wit) literally every area where I have found candidates to fall short"

—Keri Lyle, Google Recruiter

"The author provides a clear, comprehensive process to follow that will take candidates from mediocrity to standing out… I'd emphasize that this also appeals to the 'Power User'—even though I've been through this process several times, this book definitely helped me clarify my story for WHY I want a certain job, and how to get it."

—Chris Ludwick

Appreciation

I wrote this book for every person who believes they deserve to have their perfect job, but don't know where to start.

Thank you to my friends and family for the constant support and feedback as this book has progressed. A special thank you to Bo Meng, Chris Ludwick, Steve Brady and Derek Walker for their selfless editorial work, and for giving it to me straight.

I'd like to dedicate this book to my radiant wife Ameena, my family to whom I owe everything, and my grandfather who taught me the value of the three Is.

1. Introduction: You are twice as impressive as your current resume says you are

I wrote this book because, as an experienced interviewer, I have seen too many great candidates fail to make it through the resume and screening rounds of their potential dream jobs, not because of an over-supply of parental positive reinforcement, but because they simply did not prepare well enough, or fell victim to a little hubris and at least one of the three inconvenient truths:

- **Most candidates don't realize they are doing it all wrong.** They hope that the employment or academic brands on their resume will carry them through simply by listing them and some bland previous job descriptions. In my experience, the reality is that most of your competitors are sporting the same brands, if not better. I'll show you how to rise out of even the most talented field by combining your unique set of personal assets and experiences, and weaving them together to tell a coherent and powerful story.

- **Every single resume I've ever seen could be made at least twice as impressive.** This almost always entails learning how to demonstrate to the recruiter that you are the perfect fit for your desired job. I'll show you how to take your resume to the next level with some training, some honing and some targeted research.

- **Applying for a job is really, really hard work.** You will only succeed if you are willing to invest significant time researching your future company and job, significant time searching through your own thoughts and beliefs, and even more significant time fashioning all of this into a cohesive personal sales pitch that helps you stand out from the thousands of other applicants applying for the same position.

This book is as short and punchy as I could make it, because you shouldn't have to read a 400-page tome before trying to write a two-page resume. The value of this book is in the step-by-step exercises you will complete within each chapter, putting the emphasis on your thinking and on tangible output.

It's important to note that this **is not just about creating a resume or cover letter**. It is woefully insufficient to simply recount the job descriptions of roles you have occupied and hope the employer makes the right connections. Getting a job today requires distilling your personal story, matching it to each employer's needs and finding the perfect medium through which to communicate it.

If you want to get hired, you have to stand out of the crowd. Do not hope that the recruiter will piece together your mundane previous job descriptions or take a chance based on an ill-considered or irrelevant blob of dense text. Rather, **learn how to tell a compelling story of your life and career** to demonstrate depth, uniquely valuable skills and traits, and above all a perfect fit for the company and job to which you're applying.

With this book I hope to give you the confidence to apply for the job you deserve, and the knowledge and tools to get yourself noticed.

1.1. Why should you believe me?

In my time at McKinsey, Oxford and most recently Google, I have personally assessed multitudes of candidates across classic big-three-type strategy consulting (McKinsey, Bain and BCG), tech strategy and product manager interviews. I have participated in hiring committees, engaged in review discussions of hundreds of candidates, and have trained hundreds more in one-on-one and group settings. I have seen candidates of both great and terrible ilk, but those that stand out most starkly in my mind, and the vast majority that I've seen, are those that are "woefully underprepared".

While my perspective is biased towards McKinsey and Google, I have tried to generalize the basic principles that years of working across industries and functions within Fortune 500 companies has reinforced: great people understand their personal assets, how to sell them, and how to match them to the role requirements of the places they work.

1.2.   Should you read this book?

If headhunters are regularly banging down your door to attract you to the next executive-level position, then chances are there is little I can help you with.

For everyone else, the chances of you unknowingly underselling yourself are simply too high to ignore, based on the very large sample size of my recruitment and candidate training experience. Given the high stakes and the sky-high rewards, **why wouldn't you take some time to read a short book, which just may make the crucial difference** in getting you that prized interview.

The approach I lay out here instructs you in creating the best possible story for your unique situation, and therefore applies to:

- **Almost any industry and type of company**—from services firms to technical or operations companies, and from startups to large corporations.

- **Almost any job level**—from recent college graduates applying for their first job, to more senior managers/associates looking to change direction and remarket themselves to new firms or industries.

I do not offer sample resumes or a "fill-in-the-blanks" formula (though you can download a basic resume word template at standout-fitin-gethired.com), because I believe that this encourages laziness in both articulating your personal value proposition and fine-tuning it to the job at hand. In that sense, I hope this book will guide you to ask the right questions of yourself, and to distill the best possible answers to meet your goals.

1.3. What you'll have created by the end.

- **Section 2—All about you**—The perfect application starts with you. Who are you? Do you even know? Getting to grips with what you're good at, what you believe in, and what your past experiences have taught you and signal to those evaluating you, are crucial parts of your application. Too many candidates lack the confidence or thoughtfulness to articulate this adequately.

- **Section 3—All about your new dream industry, company and role**—How well do you know the industry, company and job you're applying for? If your answer isn't "almost as well as the person interviewing me", then you aren't doing enough. You should be reaching into the vastness of the blogosphere, news sites, LinkedIn and your own personal social networks to mine every morsel of information about your potential new role.

- **Section 4—Creating the perfect resume**—Turning these deep introspective thoughts and mountains of company research into a punchy and eye-catching one-pager is no small feat. I walk you step-by-step through crafting your application, including options for addressing head-on your shortcomings in terms of knowledge or experience.

- **Section 5—Defining your personal pitch**—It's one thing to have your history captured concisely on a page, but it's quite another to articulate your personal story in a short, sharp and memorable way. In this chapter we create your cover page, tying all of the previous steps together to bring color, passion and personality to your application. I also explore alternative mediums and formats.

- **Section 6—Get your resume into the right hands**—There are thousands of people applying for your dream job. What can you do to get noticed by the screeners and recruiters who are trying to identify great candidates to invite to the interview? I detail three approaches including getting yourself referred, getting noticed by senior execs, and getting found in LinkedIn and Google search results.

My challenge to you: Dedicate the time to actually work through the suggested activities in each successive chapter. By the end, you will have a sharp new resume and a punchy personal sales pitch. Take careful note of the differences between what you started with and what you have at the end of this process.

I'd love to hear your feedback on Twitter at @brandontrew, or through my blog at brandontrew.com. I'll be updating this book as often as I can in order to keep it relevant and useful, so keep an eye out for Kindle updates.

Keep an eye out for my next book on Case Interviews: I started this book as a "Case Interview" guide but quickly realized that many of the fundamentals required to succeed in the case interview have their roots in the preparation and homework that candidates should be doing before every single interview. This book has therefore been written as part one of my (still to be published) follow-up book: "The Inside Guide to Case Interviews: and how to get out of the blender", so that you can learn how to nail the interviews once you make it through the initial screening. Check inside-guides.com for more info.

CHAPTER 2

2. To stand out, you must find your inner snowflake

L et me be very clear—**a mediocre-effort resume simply isn't good enough.** Applying for an analyst / associate / product manager / leadership rotation program role at a Fortune 500, tech or consulting company is a very competitive endeavor. Hundreds, if not thousands, of top-notch applicants from around the world are vying for the same spot as you are. A run-of-the-mill application without insight, clarity and extreme focus will be completely indiscernible from other mediocre-effort candidates who have taken the same hit-and-hope approach.

The candidates you are up against are all incredibly talented and probably have a healthy dose of resume eye candy in the form of prized blue chip former employers or impressive-sounding accomplishments. However, there is something about you that gives you an advantage: a combination of unique values, experiences and skills that makes you fundamentally different and more valuable than your competitors.

If you get nothing else from this book, you should develop the ability to think through your personal value proposition, synthesize it into a punchy set of benefits, and express it in such a way that recruiters want to bring you in for a personal interview.

> **OUTPUT - By the end of this chapter, you will have:**
>
> 1. An understanding of the exact characteristics your recruiter will evaluate you against.
>
> 2. The ability to articulate your core values.
>
> 3. Turned a list of work experiences into attractive list of benefits that your employer will value.

2.1. Five characteristics your potential employers are looking for you to prove in your application.

Most companies I have been involved with over the years **look for the same five essential characteristics and attributes in candidates** (although they may call it different things, and apply them to different areas and functions). You have to convince them, with just a few short interactions, that you possess qualities in all these areas:

1. **Raw ability / intelligence**—Often evaluated by looking at your school results, your awards, or the caliber of previous companies you have worked for.

    This criterion looks at your intrinsic qualities to see if you are: a clear and logical thinker; a concise and crisp communicator; strong with numbers and analytical concepts; able to grasp new concepts easily.

2. **Experience / role-related knowledge**—This is evaluated based on the description of your work experience, and through experiential questions during the interview process. You have to demonstrate to the interviewer that you can meet or exceed every role requirement in the job description.

There must be no doubt in the interviewer's mind that you tick all of the most important knowledge and experience boxes. It is your job to clearly signpost these, to make them easily recognizable.

3. **Cultural "fit" / personality**—You have to be aligned with the culture and values of both the overall company and business unit to which you are applying. This entails doing as much homework as possible about the kinds of people you will be working with, and the expectations of how you will interact, communicate, and socialize with other people in your team, both horizontally (peers across all teams you will deal with) and vertically (both direct reports and managers) (see Chapter 3.1.3).

    This also includes demonstrating the company's alignment with your own values and your priorities, which in turn requires a lot of careful introspection and asking yourself the right questions (see Chapter 2.2.1). Be really honest with yourself about how your beliefs would fit in with those of your target company. Providing examples of how you have worked and achieved in similar environments is key.

4. **Leadership** – Typically broken down into three different categories:

    4.1. **Thought leadership**—Provide examples of times you have taken ownership of a problem, broken it into subcomponents, and led a team in solving it. Add extra emphasis to times when you have identified new opportunities or innovations, and driven a team to find a solution. Were you able to apply areas of expertise you possess to influence the team's direction?

    4.2. **Team leadership**—This is fluffier. Do you have examples of cases where you created positive, enthusiastic and productive team environments? Find examples that demonstrate your approach and commitment to mentorship and the development of those below and around you. For younger candidates without experience in managing teams, this can also involve leading by example.

4.3.   **Client/partner leadership** – This is often referred to as the ability to become a "trusted advisor" to a client or partner. Demonstrate ways a client or partner has trusted you, in addition to paying for your services. Have they sought advice on matters unrelated to your current project? Were you able to influence their decision-making using your relationship and knowledge?

5.   **Spark**—Many recruiters I know at McKinsey and Google start reading a resume from the bottom. The "interests" category is one of the few areas on your resume where you can demonstrate what makes you interesting and unique as a candidate, yet too many applicants leave this section entirely empty.

The firms you're applying to want to see that you're a person with passions, not just another corporate clone: someone who can identify a problem (in society, in business, in your college, etc.), and find and implement a solution independently. You need to have at least one "lightning rod" in that category—the one thing you're most proud of and which you would say, on your deathbed, was what made you a special snowflake. It doesn't have to be fancy, but it does have to show the living, breathing and more interesting side of you.

2.2.   Develop your story, before you do anything else.

It's easy to spot a terrible salesperson. They either don't believe in what they are selling, or have no idea what it is they are selling in the first place. This is alarmingly common in candidates I've seen and leaves me wondering why they bothered to apply at all. If you don't believe you're good enough to work somewhere, you have no chance of convincing a recruiter or interviewer that they should consider you.

Before you can sell yourself, you have to know yourself. This can be really difficult, especially if you aren't sure what you want or where you want to be. But without it, you are going to have a hard time finding willing buyers.

2.2.1. Start with what you believe in (and what you don't).

Think of a couple of your friends that work for investment banks, consulting firms, NGOs, or large corporate employers. Chances are you could identify patterns in personality and values between these companies and industries that are not coincidental.

It is very easy to identify a company's values from the kinds of people they hire, and the kinds of people their employees become over time.

Understanding this two-way interaction, from employees to company culture, and from company culture back towards employees, is an important part of the interview process—I've heard a few recruiters say something along the lines of "give me a smart candidate that fits our culture, and everything else will fall into place".

The first step in your application process should be to identify what you believe in:

- Where does your moral/business compass point on issues of meritocracy, conflict resolution, posturing and bullying, delegation, consensus building, and workplace humor (just to name a few)?

  Finish sentences such as "Someone disagrees with me publicly at work so I…" and "I want to convince a peer to take a course of action they do not initially support, so I…".

- How far are you prepared to push yourself and your loved ones to succeed at your job in terms of work hours, travel and work-life balance, or weekend emails?

- If a new opportunity presents itself, how aggressively would you pursue it? What if somebody tried to block you?

- Are you a builder or a maintainer?

- Do you prefer a hierarchy with command-and-control decision making, or a flat structure involving building consensus?

- How do you feel about taking responsibility—would you rather ask for permission or forgiveness? Are you comfortable with big risks and big rewards?

- What is your preference for dealing with confrontation? Are you willing to speak your mind around a heated boardroom?

- Should you push to make as much money as possible out of a client from each contract, or share more of the value with the client to develop long term but less immediately profitable relationships?

There are no right answers. There are only your answers. And it is very easy to spot when someone is faking. **Don't try to tell the interviewer what you think they want to hear.** Your best bet in an interview is to be upfront about all of these things, giving examples of where you stood up for what you believed.

2.2.2. Identify your personal career assets, and make them shine.

Why should I hire you?

What are you really good at?

What would you be better than anyone else at?

Prove it.

There's no sugarcoating it. Those are the questions that every recruiter is looking for you to answer. When you calculate the value of a company, the first thing you do is identify its value-generating assets, and then you try and figure out how much each of those assets is worth.

In the "bad old days" of consumer electronics marketing, mobile phone makers would try to differentiate based on a slightly tweaked keypad layout, or a new messaging feature, or the speed of the processor. Only people didn't want those things, because they had no idea how they would impact their lives. Apple sold customers a promise and a vision of how their lives would be better because of Apple's technology. Rather than system specs, Apple ads emphasized the daily activities that people aspire to perform everyday, like composing a musical score or having a video chat with their young child. Apple highlighted amazing new features that looked incredibly simple and beautiful and people could see themselves wanting to perform those actions in the future. Apple is amongst the best in the world at packaging beauty and tangible benefits, which is why it's no coincidence that at the time of publication they were the world's most valuable company.

The same lesson can be applied to your job application. As a salesperson, one of the first lessons you learn is that **customers buy benefits, not features**. It is very hard to identify the value in a resume that reads like a laundry list of seemingly unrelated job tasks. Instead, your personal story needs to be built around a coherent collage of your personal value-creating assets—the benefits your future employer will receive when they hire you.

Look back over the list of activities, roles and projects you have been involved with at each company or organization you have worked for or school you have attended:

- Focus on remembering and refining all the activities you took part in, and in particular the achievements or outcomes you drove to conclusion (versus what the project team or group did).

- What compact nuggets of experience and/or knowledge did you derive from projects or activities, and which of these "assets" within your personal story jump out and complement each other?

- How do they match up to the five criteria mentioned in the previous chapter?

- What have you built or launched?

- What specialist knowledge have you collected from these experiences?

- Why have your former organizations been richer and better off thanks to your involvement?

Find the three things you know you are best at, and can demonstrate using your personal story. And tell me why the unique combination of those three things makes you more valuable than any other candidate. These are the assets that you need to pull out, package and prepare in your own mind to sell to your potential employer in a short, sharp and confident way.

Know your audience. You need to understand the perceived value judgments of the people you're pitching to when crafting your message—for example, Guy Kawasaki is on record as saying that he estimates the value of a startup by adding $100,000 for each MBA, and $1 million for each engineer (although his specific values have shifted depending where it was reported, his principle remains the same). In my own experience, I know many Silicon Valley recruiters who believe that an MBA is a black mark on a resume (full disclosure, I have one), especially for startups and tech companies. Here the belief is that real-world experience in execution beats "management training" which emphasizes the strategic at the expense of the tactical. This is not my belief, but be aware that if you have an MBA then you will face this stigma in certain industries, so toning this down and emphasizing your more technical or executional talents would stand you in better stead.

Other forms of qualification snobbery may, rightly or wrongly, affect you in other industries or areas, so making yourself aware of these stigmas can help you avoid obvious pitfalls. Do your homework and adjust the emphasis on each skill set appropriately.

CHAPTER 3

3. Become an expert on your prospective company and role

The "shotgun" approach, in which you create one general passable resume and broadcast it to every application site you can find **is guaranteed not to get you the job you want.**

Interviewers at top companies are like needy boyfriends or girlfriends—they need to be told regularly that you are truly, madly, and deeply devoted only to them, and that you want to be there for the "right reasons" (which never includes money, the company's brand name, using that position as a stepping stone to somewhere else, or other answers of an equally uninspired nature). This means that every piece of communication and every story should reinforce the single-minded goal of getting that job. It's conceited. It's unrealistic. But you better believe it's important to get this pitch perfect.

Your job is to optimize the various mediums at your disposal—resume/CV, references, work history, personal interests, work anecdotes, and case interviews—to convince the HR person screening your application packet that they should give you a chance. In order to achieve this, you first need to understand what makes them tick in exquisite detail.

OUTPUT - By the end of this Chapter, you will have:

1. **A deep and insightful understanding of the industry,** company business model, company culture, and employees' perspectives of the company to which you're applying.

2. **Answered the question: "Do I really want to work there?"**

3. **A detailed and comprehensive list of all job requirements** you will be evaluated against in order to grant you an interview.

3.1. Recruiters and interviewers expect you to know as much about their company as they do.

Your interviews are conducted by employees who are very deeply immersed in their day-to-day jobs. Although they are instructed to give you the benefit of the doubt in terms of prior knowledge, subliminally they are likely to be much more excited about you as a candidate if you are able to identify the core issues they work with every day, and comment with some level of insight on them.

Being extremely knowledgeable about their company also signals that you are someone who is interested in the industry and takes the job application very seriously, immediately helping you to stand out of the crowd. At some of the companies I've worked for, not knowing how much the company made in revenue the previous year is almost a sure way to get rejected immediately.

Here is a starter list of questions you should minimally be able to answer using sources like the company investor relations site, Quora, LinkedIn, WetFeet, or general web searches for people's blogged experiences with those companies.

3.1.1. Become an industry expert, quickly.

*   How big is the industry?

- Who are the main players?

- Who are the up-and-comers?

- How do they differentiate themselves?

- What would they say about each other?

- What happened in the industry in the last year / few months that really matters?

- Where is the industry going?

- Why is that exciting?

- What about the answers above attracts you to this industry and entices you?

3.1.2. Know your dream company's business model(s) inside-out.

- Read the 10k / annual report. Twice. In particular focus on the strategy section, the description of current products, and the earnings information.

- Go and find four high-profile blogs that like to write about that company—two staunch proponents and two staunch opponents.

- What is that company's strategic position in the industry?

- What makes them strong or weak and what should they do to fix it?

- Where are they going as a company?

- What are the big rumors?

- What are the main revenue streams and key company metrics? (Hint: for Google this includes revenue, cost per click, and query growth rate, amongst other things).

- Which business units provide most of that revenue?

- Which business units interest you, and for what reasons?

3.1.3. Know your dream company's culture inside-out.

- How would you describe an employee from that company, based on anecdotes you've heard or experiences with people you've met?

- How would they describe themselves or differentiate themselves from employees at other companies?

- What do you admire about their approach and their culture?

- Does this company make decisions by command-and-control or consensus?

- What personal employee attributes are most rewarded?

- What do the employees you've contacted value most about the company culture?

- Look for evidence of action: public statements, charitable giving, and discussions on Quora.

3.1.4. Get to know the people in your potential team.

LinkedIn offers access to people in the team to which you are applying:

- Who are they and what did they do before working there?

- How long have they been there?

- What are their interests?

- What is similar and different about the different team members?

- What kind of person would they love to have join the team?

- Once you know who your interviewers will be, research them in depth using Google and LinkedIn.

3.2. Establish your North Star—make a list of <u>all</u> of the role requirements.

Now that you understand the company enough to discuss intricate details with current employees, you need to understand exactly what they are looking for in you. By the time the interviewer has finished a single read-through of your resume, they must be able to establish that all the important items on their role requirements list are ticked, as well as their list of required personal characteristics from Chapter 2.2.1.

At times many of the job requirements may be only vaguely described or are not publicly disclosed in the official job description at all. This can happen for any number of reasons including secret projects, heavily entrenched corporate culture requirements, or a lack of detail provided by the hiring manager. Nevertheless, these requirements are well codified by the recruiters and interviewers, and are therefore something you're expected to demonstrate.

Your next task is to develop the most detailed list of requirements you can from public, social, and unofficial sources.

3.2.1. Publicly available job information.

- Job title and description.

- Reporting line and business unit.

- Products or activities your prospective team is focused on.

- Day-to-day tasks and responsibilities.

- Detailed minimum requirements.

3.2.2. Trickier organizational information related to the role.

- What personal character traits does the organization admire and nurture? You better believe they are on the list.

- What career ladder does the role fall into? This often determines your career path, your peers and your mentors. But it also establishes the "core career competencies" that you are expected to master to progress through that ladder (all of which are on the list).

- Against which explicit criteria would your performance be evaluated? This is often not clear from the job description.

- Which other groups will you be working closely with, and what traits are they looking for and evaluating you against?

- What are the power dynamics between the roles?

3.2.3. "Real world" requirements not captured in the official description (unpublished).

- Job descriptions often don't take into account the much richer nuances of what makes a good or bad employee in that role. You can only get this information from talking to actual people in those roles. Write down everything required to succeed.

- Political / relationship / interpersonal skills required to succeed at that company—some companies will require you to have mastered a whole set of interpersonal skills in order to be able to perform your daily tasks (but these won't be listed on the job description). Find out how you are expected to influence people and get things done (draw this from your research on company culture in Chapter 3.1.3).

Only some of the real world requirements will be public (and not necessarily in the job description) and you will need to do a lot of reading up on blogs and unofficial websites, and networking through friends of friends and online in order to discover the whole truth. However by doing this you will also have the opportunity to do some reverse screening to decide whether your target company is somewhere you would actually like to work.

Once you've gathered as much information as you can, collate all of it into a final and detailed list of requirements. In the next chapter, I will show you how to construct a personal story that maximizes your chance of proving to the recruiter and interviewer that you meet or exceed their expectations.

CHAPTER 4

4. Stand out with a resume hyper-tailored for every job

There is some debate about whether you should craft the resume first and your personal sales pitch (Chapter 5) second, or the other way around. My opinion is that your resume should be completed first, since it provides the factual basis on which to build the more colorful and subjective personal sales pitch. This approach also forces you to first spend time facing your own reality—the raw facts of your achievements and finished projects throughout your life—and then identifying the roles that best suit what you uniquely have to offer.

Like it or not, careers are unfortunately highly path-dependent, meaning that your future trajectory is inextricably tied to what you have done in the past. I guarantee you that choosing a path that best fits the assets you have built so far is the smoothest path to getting hired. If you want to change industries, functions and/or locations (known as "the Triple Jump" if done all at once) then you have a significant hill to climb. Not to sound gloomy, but I can't say this strongly enough; while you have every right to try (in which case the following chapters will still serve you well), you will have your work cut out for you. Hope is not entirely lost however as I outline a number of strategies in Chapter 4.8 for how best to tackle a change in direction.

Assuming that you've chosen a company and role that fits your experiences to date, your next step is to prepare your resume and application, which the rest of this chapter will cover in detail. Depending on whom you're trying to impress, **a standard resume may not be the best approach.** I will deal with alternative formats in Chapter 5.3. I recommend you still go through this chapter though, since the process of matching your experience to the job requirements, and conveying them in an attractive way, are still the crucial step in getting a job.

OUTPUT - By the end of this Chapter, you will have:

1. **Been honest with yourself about whether you meet the minimum skill, experience and other requirements or not,** and plotted an alternative track to get what you want if the answer is "no".

2. **Understood the importance of optimizing for the single skim-read experience of your resume.**

3. **Rewritten your past activities in terms of Quantified High Impact Results in Punchy Bullet points.**

4. **Identified gaps in your application** using the Requirements-Characteristics matrix.

5. **Optimized your resume to get past the filters of the Applicant Tracking System (ATS)**

6. **Formatted your resume** to lead your recruiter's eyes to the most important points on the page.

7. **Checked that a total layman could easily understand everything in your resume** and could agree that you have ticked off each of the job requirements from above.

4.1. You will be evaluated on <u>one skim-read</u>. Make it count.

Throughout the application, remember that the gatekeeper to your future is the HR recruiter or resume screener. They are making the decisions that will affect the rest of your life, and they are doing so based on a single skim-read of your resume. That's all you have. One skim-read. Anything superfluous, irrelevant or not specifically supporting your "hiring story" is simply distracting the interviewer, or worse, boring them.

4.1.1. Skip the personal details section. Skip the personal statement.

Don't waste valuable space on irrelevant personal fluff. You only need enough personal contact information so that your interviewer can identify you in the stack, and call/email you back. Mostly, they will already have your contact details through the general application form. Only include information such as nationality, languages, immigration status, etc., if it is directly pertinent to the application.

I'm also not a fan of **personal statements** (the fluffy opening paragraph some people like to add to their resumes). They tend to be short on well-supported facts, and heavy on unsubstantiated assertions, and have the overall impact of reducing the credibility of your application. This is a matter of personal preference though, so if you really want to add one then make sure that each statement you make is well supported and that it references the same talking points as the rest of the resume. Some argue that this section helps with ATS resume scanning (see Chapter 4.5), however most systems look for keyword matches across your whole resume, so strengthening your other sections makes more sense in my opinion. **I strongly prefer conveying your "sales pitch" through consistent and very well articulated bullet point descriptions** throughout the resume, where the main points should jump off the page and be well substantiated.

4.1.2. Education or work experience first?

Your recruiter wants to know that you have the minimum qualification required. It does not matter if your education section is above or below your work experience section, unless you have some unique circumstances that may tilt towards one or the other:

If you do not have the minimum level of formal qualification but you do have industry experience sufficient to demonstrate the skills and knowledge, then you should talk about the experience first, so that there is no doubt that they should proceed with you by the time the recruiter reads about your qualifications.

If you do not meet the minimum industry experience requirement, but you have an advanced degree with deep specialist knowledge (like a doctoral degree), then you should talk about your education first, since this stresses the higher levels of thinking and maturity you bring, over other applicants with a similar level of work experience only.

4.1.3. "I just left college, and I don't have any of this fancy stuff".

If you're fresh out of college, then chances are you're applying for a job with high intellect, cultural fit and spark requirements, but very low emphasis on role-related knowledge or experience (see Chapter 2.1 for details). Use the job requirements as a guide here.

Always find ways to differentiate yourself: Even at college, you have to get cracking finding and exploring something you are passionate about and which differentiates you from others (see Chapter 4.1.5 on lightning rods). Grades are not sufficient to get you noticed. They only tick one box (and besides, there are always smarter applicants).

Helping out at a soup kitchen will also do nothing for you. Recruiters are looking to see that you have drive, can take initiative, and are multi-faceted. So think bigger when it comes to these differentiators, and get busy. The sooner you start down this road, the easier it will be to tell a consistent story in your resume and personal pitch.

4.1.4. Weave your entire history since leaving high school into a coherent and continuous "learning pathway".

Don't leave anything out. Every month between leaving school and the present should be accounted for. If you did a gap year, or a year of travel, then include that in the "Interests" section. Most importantly, you need to tie this history together into a coherent fabric, whose logical next step is applying to your dream company.

Even if you did randomly jump around or took completely disconnected steps, **creating a storyline out of these is critical to demonstrating why your dream company makes sense as the "next step"**. This storyline should also be constructed to demonstrate both interest and passion. Employers want driven individuals who know what they want and work to achieve it. Being able to say: "I thought I had a passion for X, pursued it and realized that it was not for me", is a reasonable way of explaining inconsistencies or big jumps. Most of all, you need to ensure that the pathway to applying to that specific company and position are clear and logical. Don't lie. But definitely take the editorial license afforded to you in being able to recount your own history.

4.1.5. To prove that you're interesting, you need a lightning rod.

Employees of top companies want to work with people they respect, admire and find interesting. Recruiters look for non-work-related signals to recognize this.

Many recruiters (myself included) **actually start reading your resume at the bottom,** hence the Lightning Rod analogy (something to attract immediate attention). A person's extramural interests are a good way of assessing whether you are the kind of candidate that goes the extra mile, takes risks, or explores passions and interests. Candidates that do not take the time to describe other things that make them tick, can come across as being too one-dimensional, which gets you very few points in the "spark" area.

Take the time to think through the non-work things you like doing, especially if you have experienced some success or achieved some accolade as a result.

4.1.6. The importance of going the extra mile because you saw an opportunity, rather than because it was your job.

Recruiters don't actually expect to know you or understand you by reading your resume. What they rely on are signals that you possess the qualities they are after. One of the main qualities I've observed recruiters look for is the ability to take initiative (also known as drive, ambition, entrepreneurialism, or "spark"). The best examples of this involve demonstrating the ability to "see an opportunity or a need, start something, and execute it", not because your boss told you to or because it's part of your job description, but rather because you identified that it just needed to get done.

Any new thing you dreamed up and successfully executed on can be used to articulate this point. Businesses or NGOs you started, fund-raising you did, standard processes at any organization that you identified as inefficient and changed for the better. Be creative with things you've done. But make it clear that you took initiative! And throw in examples of this throughout your education and work experience. Merely being "President of the [*insert not particularly important sounding student body*] at school" demonstrates nothing. So be careful to add real things with real outcomes, rather than just titles.

4.1.7. Don't overdo buzzwords and jargon.

Make each line in your resume accessible to any layperson that might read it. Most recruiters are not qualified or experienced in the field to which you're applying, therefore will not be able to understand nuances in highly technical and complicated descriptions of things you've done. The recruiter must be able to understand your resume before they can be impressed by it.

Having said that, you also have to strike a balance with the use of technical terminology and common industry descriptions, since those are the things that will be flagged by the ATS system scanning your resume when it is first submitted (see Chapter 4.5 for a full description of how to get past the ATS scanning stage).

4.1.8. Don't lie. Don't embellish. Stick to the facts.

Recruiters and hiring committees are incredibly suspicious of embellished claims. And they take a very dim view of liars. They are also typically very well connected and are familiar with the rating systems of most schools and companies. It is easy to spot a fib, and just as easy to do a quick investigation to disprove suspicious claims.

Be prepared to talk about everything in your resume in great detail. While sitting around a table with some of my recruiting friends, I have heard countless stories of interviewers suspecting mistruths, digging deeper to uncover the truth, and then either outright banning the candidate or embarrassing them during an interview to teach them a lesson.

Along the same line, avoid over-the-top adjectives or unsubstantiated self-compliments. Calling yourself "talented", "exceptional", "committed", "enthusiastic", "effective", "motivated" does not make it true (see LinkedIn's post on this for more examples). Rather let these qualities emerge from your factual descriptions of things you have done. Such assertions really hurt your credibility by making you sound not terribly self-aware, and make it harder to take your claims seriously.

Don't lie. Ever. Don't embellish. Just stick to the facts. And know them cold when you step into your interview.

4.2. Forget about titles. Forget what your team did. Quantify the impact <u>you</u> had.

Probably the biggest mistake I see in resumes is applicants who try to claim individual credit for something that is clearly a broad team activity, within which they were only an insignificant cog. Equally unhelpful to your cause is brandishing impressive-sounding-but-obviously-hollow titles. Being a VP, or a "lead", or a "president" means absolutely nothing to the person reading your resume if they have no contextual understanding of the importance of that role within that organization. They certainly don't confer on the reader the confidence that the role requirements (the boxes they're mentally ticking) are actually being ticked.

The second resume pitfall I see a lot is the old logical fallacy:

- (a) VPs at X companies typically do Y;

- (b) I am a VP; therefore

- (c) I have done Y.

Unfortunately it's really obvious from these kinds of general descriptions that you have not, in fact, done what you are claiming, or at best that you were peripherally involved with the outcome in question. It is your responsibility to drive this home with the recruiter, by coming up with tangible descriptions of the things you've done and **focusing on quantifying the impact that your specific involvement had on the outcome.**

By all means discuss what your team accomplished, but demonstrate with details how your actions supported that team goal. Be modest where modesty is due—you probably didn't really cause your company to earn $2 billion extra, but you may well have done some complex analysis to identify $100 million in potential savings for a client and helped them execute the recommendations.

4.3. Rewrite your resume for each job using laser-focused HIRIP Bullets (sorry what?).

In describing the intricate and important detail of your entire career, you face a careful balancing act—describe your roles in enough detail to convince the interviewer you rock the Casbah, without being so wordy that you put them to sleep while trying to read it.

The answer lies in **HIRIP Bullets—High Impact Results In Punchy Bulletpoints**:

- **Bullet points**—Long, dense paragraphs are the surest way to get your resume ignored. Your recruiter is reading through hundreds of them every day. They are tired and under significant pressure to meet quotas. But they are looking for that faint glint of the diamond in the rough, because they are compensated to find you and get you through the process successfully.

For each role and activity in your career you need to convey the awesome things you did and achieved in the fewest possible bullet points, and with the fewest possible words.

- **High impact**—"Created presentations" is hardly eye catching. "Created numerous presentations used in board and senior executive meetings" actually sounds like you were useful. Don't bother listing the menial tasks, especially not separately.

  If you are trying to establish a set of table-stakes requirements, like "you are well organized", then rather wrap these in much more complex tasks that drive the same point home, such as "coordinated a dispersed and cross-functional team through daily task accounting, stand-up meetings and creating weekly update reports".

- **Quantified results**—Every single bullet point must have an outcome attached to it. This outcome should be measurable and quantified through some intuitive metric if at all possible, though qualitative outcomes will suffice for some activities.

  Think of how you would append some variation of "resulting in…" to every single bullet point in your resume. What really makes you stand out is providing a sense of the scope and scale of what you did, and how important your actions were for your employer/ client.

- **Punchy**—Write out the description, including the high impact and quantified results components. Now challenge yourself to take out half of the words. Read it again. And take out another few words. This takes work (hence the old adage by Bernard Shaw: "I'm sorry this letter is so long, I didn't have time to make it shorter").

  The result should be no more than two lines. Your recruiter should be able to say the sentence in one breath, hold all of the key concepts in mind at once, and spot the keywords within the text. Make their job easy here, and you will reap the rewards.

Rinse and repeat this process for any activity, role, or other big-ticket item on your resume, including education, clubs, or hobbies that really stand out.

4.4. How does your application stack up against the evaluation criteria? Visualize it.

Put yourself in your recruiter's shoes—very little time, a lot of content to read, and a list of requirements they have to identify before letting you through the gate. You maximize your chance of being accepted if you ensure that, broadly across your entire resume, you cover each of the requirements at least once, preferably twice, and even three times for the obviously most important requirements.

Complete <u>the Characteristics-Requirements (CharReq) matrix</u> to assess your application's strengths and weaknesses:

1. Take a sheet of blank paper and create six columns.

2. Label each column, the first being "requirements", followed by the five characteristic groups I described in Chapter 2.1 (intelligence, role-related knowledge, culture fit, leadership and spark).

3. In the first column write down all of your job requirements, plus everything else you know from your research in Chapter 3. Synthesize this into logical requirements groupings with one new row for each group.

4. Now think about your employment/education history and plot each task, job or activity you have performed into this matrix. You can enhance this further by making the dot larger or smaller based on how much weight you think each point will carry, based on its duration, complexity or significance. Once you're done, take a step back. Where do you have a lot of clustering? Which blocks are really light on content? Which blocks don't actually make sense, and can be disregarded?

5. Your recruiter is performing this exercise in their heads—they are adding up all the points in each row, and each column, and deciding if you pass the bar.

6. To fill in some of the gaps, either try to find examples you had previously forgotten to mention, or reframe some of your existing points to expand the requirements they cover. At the end of the exercise, you should have as much of the map covered as possible, with a higher density in the rows or columns that your employer clearly cares most about.

Here's an example of a dummy CharReq matrix I put together for a Consultant position, to give you a sense of what it could look like:

Dummy Consultant CharReq	Intelligence	Role-related Knowledge	Culture fit	Leadership	Spark
Req 1 – Solve ambiguous problems	PhD in X from Y	4 years as EIR at venture fund		N / A	Startup during university doing Y
Req 2 – Build client relationships	N / A		Mentor at XX program		
Req 3 – Conduct complex analysis	Cluster analysis within PhD		1 yr internship doing "Moneyball" for the Blue Jays		Used model to assess market size in startup
Req 4 – Contribute to broader firm				Taught yoga	Extensive travels
Req 5 – Present to senior execs					

In this example, although clearly very accomplished, many of the pertinent boxes remain empty, or insufficiently covered. At this point, it would be worth revisiting the activities performed within each role, position, or academic endeavor, and tweaking them to more directly address the gaps. For example, this candidate could highlight any public speaking they had done at conferences or while pitching venture capitalists as an Entrepreneur-in-Residence. They should also look to bolster their leadership story with specific examples of leading teams or projects. Making the connection between a past role and meeting a requirement isn't always obvious to the recruiter trying to make sense of all this, so you should make it crystal clear in your bullet points.

If you find you have a lot of examples of the same task clustered into the same box, then try to find a way to convey each requirement in an interesting and unique way, preferably from different perspectives that demonstrate you understand the space in depth. One approach you could take here is to describe tasks that span two different characteristics, for example combining role-related knowledge and leadership (e.g. you trained someone in a specific activity that you had previously mastered in a previous similar role).

If you were an analyst / engineer at three companies (or had three roles within a company), then make sure you find three different and complementary examples in which you performed the same activity. Describe each one in order to demonstrate an increasing level of mastery and impact. This is a great opportunity to show you are (a) an expert, but more importantly (b) you learn fast and take feedback well as you grow.

4.5. Getting past the digital gatekeeper—the Applicant Tracking System.

I strongly recommend that you never simply submit your resume to a company's online application tool if you can help it (see Chapter 6 for the approaches I do recommend). Not only are you placed in a giant vat with a seemingly endless number of other hopeful and indistinguishable candidates, but you're also subject to a range of fairly random and typically automated screening steps by systems known as Applicant Tracking Systems (ATS).

For those of you that are unable to find a better application pathway, this chapter will deal with how to construct an ATS-friendly resume. However I want to emphasize that the ATS is just the first gatekeeper. **A human still has to read and like your resume after this before inviting you to an interview**, so don't sacrifice the rest of the tips in this chapter for the sake of making it past the automated screening. While it takes some thought, achieving both outcomes should not be mutually exclusive.

It is estimated that around 50 percent of large and medium companies use an ATS in order to sort, scan, filter, and manage the large numbers of resumes they receive each year. This means once you have uploaded your resume, the system automatically scans and ranks it with a relevance score based on matching your resume text to the job description to which you are applying. Most of these systems are not very smart, and for the most part rely on plain vanilla keyword matching. The smarter systems look at the context around those keywords to see if what you've written makes sense in context.

CIO magazine estimates that up to 75 percent of ATS-discarded resumes are for reasons more linked with formatting and incorrect parsing of the resume than to the applicant's candidacy. You have to take advantage of how these systems work in order to make it through the first checkpoint.

4.5.1. Avoiding the common ATS rejection pitfalls.

Probably the most common issue is that **ATS' don't understand complex formatting or images**, and consequently cannot understand and rank your resume. In most cases this will relegate your application to the never-read resume graveyard.

To ensure you are not a victim of this, limit your formatting to:

- A standard font: Arial, Georgia, Impact, Courier, Lucinda, Palatino, Verdana, Sans Serif, Tahoma, Trebuchet.

- Simple use of regular formatting, with **bold for emphasis**.

- Basic bullet points only (no fancy arrows, stars or images).

- Basic text alignment (justify, left, center, right).

- Don't use tables, floating boxes, or other design tricks—ATS systems tend to read those top to bottom rather than left to right as a human would.

- Avoid specialist formatting with lines or shading where possible.

When submitting your resume, **the document type also makes a difference** to how easily the system can parse it:

- Submit your resume in DOC or RTF format, since those are most reliably parsed. Avoid PDFs or even DOCX formats.

- Give your file a logical and clear name: [first name][last name]-[resume]-[month-year].doc so that if it ends up on your recruiters desktop, they can easily tell what it is.

4.5.2. Use common section conventions that the ATS expects and can understand.

- **Use common and standard names for each of your sections** - ATS' look for this in order to parse (read) your resume and understand what your bullet points mean: "Work Experience", "Education" or "Qualifications", "Interests" or "Achievements", and "Skills". Less sophisticated systems still do not understand more nuanced sections like "Publications" or "Conferences attended".

- **Most ATS' look for a reverse chronological order of events and activities,** and look for specific metadata per entry—specifically "company, role, duration" in that order. Make sure you include all this information for each entry. ATS systems parse out the time spent within each role and attempt to score these entries based on experience, so make sure that this is clear and in-line with each role entry.

4.5.3. Keywords, keywords, keywords.

"Keywords are the nouns and noun phrases used by
recruiters searching through applicant databases and
Web job sites for resumes meeting the requirements
on job descriptions" **- Susan P. Joyce, job-hunt.org**

• **Make sure that you use all of the most important keywords from the job description** you're targeting, as well as keywords from other relevant sections of the company's recruiting collateral, since those are the first keywords the system will scan for.

• **Include both the full name of abbreviated/acronym terms, then add the abbreviation or acronym in brackets,** for example "Sarbanes Oxley (SOX)". As described in Chapter 4.1.7, ensure that a layperson can still understand your points by making the descriptions more accessible where possible.

• **ATS' don't understand the underlying meaning of words you choose,** therefore they can't match synonyms or similar concepts. Include different terms for the same thing if necessary to ensure an ATS successfully matches your bullet point.

• **Differentiate yourself from other candidates by including other keywords that show your depth and breadth—**ATS' reward this by increasing your ranking (provided the other keywords are useful in context). For example "certified physiotherapist" may rank higher than "physiotherapist".

• **ATS' don't respond well to "keyword blocks"—**this looks like you're trying to game the system. Make sure you include all of these keywords in their correct context throughout your resume. Even worse, don't hide a whole lot of keywords in white text (or something similar) just to obviously try and fool the system.

4.5.4. Make a keyword cloud to find the keywords you should be using.

One of the best tips I've I can give you, is to copy and dump all text from the job description and other recruitment collateral for your target company and role into a word cloud generator such as http://tagcrowd.com or http://tagul.com—this will generate an infographic for you that strips out unnecessary words, and emphasizes the most important ones using size and color.

    As an example, I took all available online recruiting material for a McKinsey analyst or associate position and used tagul.com to create the visual word cloud on the following page. Can you guess what you should be emphasizing in your resume through your choice of concepts and keywords? How about "serving and putting the client first", "bringing fresh ideas to problem-solving", and "presenting recommendations based on industry knowledge, data and analytical conclusions"?

4.5.5. Bolster your credibility for technical roles.

For technical roles that require knowledge of and experience with specific tools, make sure you explicitly list these in a separate "Skills" section. Examples of this include specific tools such as "Java", "Objective C", or "combine harvester", or specific standards you have been rated against such as "ISO9000".

Using a multi-column layout in this case is acceptable since the system will match the keywords and the main purpose of this section is to improve your ATS ranking relevance. However in order to impress a human reader, the onus is still on you to demonstrate through the bullet points in your job descriptions both where, and to what degree, you learned and utilized these proficiencies within your previous roles.

4.6. Think "design and flow", not "formatting and layout".

Truth be told, nobody cares what font you use (... well... apart from comic sans). Nor do they care if you have a tasteful herringbone background to the "Education" and "Work Experience" header bars or not. **Some industries do have specific templates they expect you to have completed**—the finance world is notorious for this, so check with the recruiter before submitting—but generally speaking, recruiters just want your resume to be as short and as readable as possible. I've included a basic starter-template at www.standout-fitin-gethired. com.

From an overworked recruiter's perspective, the only thing they really care about is the ease with which they can skim-read your resume, and the way your layout guides their eyes to the key criteria they are using to assess you.

The difference between a good and a bad resume can be summarized in a few key design points:

- **Give your reader a quick-and-easy 30,000-foot view**—allow your reader to take in your whole story at a glance. Try moving the page away from your face. Further. Far enough to be unable to make out the details in the paragraphs. What can you make out? If your dense blobs of text look like a series of gray boxes, it needs work.

  What they should see as they move further away is the "top level story"—your name should be crystal clear at any distance (to create an association with you as a person), as should the number of organizations you studied and worked at. They should also see that you have a lightning rod (see Chapter 4.1.5) and that there was clear personal growth in the roles as you advanced, as judged by your title and the length of tasks and jobs.

  Create visual distinctions through the combination of font size and boldness to highlight companies, titles and sections, so that a reader immediately gets a sense of what you're made of at a glance.

- **One piece of paper is all you're allowed**—having to page through your resume will instantly kill your chances. Apart from making a 30,000-foot view impossible (humans can't robustly visualize this much information in their heads at once), this also sends the message to your recruiter that you are unable to synthesize your information into the most important points.

  Your goal is to tick all of the recruiter's boxes, ideally with just a few keywords. Add just enough by way of descriptions and numbers to add color and credibility to your claims. For view-ability, one page is generally better than two pages (depending on your level of experience), so try your best to stick to that.

- **Whitespace is not "wasted space"**—it gives the eyes a break, it allows you to direct the eyes of the recruiter to key points, and it helps logically separate roles or events chronologically. But only if you leave some white space.

- **Draw the eyes to key points using dark bold text**—try reading your resume in 10 seconds. Which words did your eyes jump to? Which words would you have liked them to have jumped to? Make those words bold, but be selective or your eyes won't be able to find them. Keep doing the 10-second test until you see the right points.

- **Highlight the continuous timeline**—recruiters tend to care about continuity between leaving school and the present. You do yourself a lot of favors if you make this obvious in the design of your resume. Add the dates down the left hand side, for example, and indent the content to the right, so that the natural direction of the eye can compare the sequence of dates, before appending to each one the role held.

- **Large, bold name and simple, smaller contact details (email and phone) at the very top of the page**—your resume will often be stacked with many others. You want to make it simple to thumb or riffle through the pages and distinguish your details instantly.

4.7. How do you know when it's good enough? Pass the layman test.

As a general rule, your resume will be ready when:

1. It is as simple as you can possibly make it, without fluff or jargon.

2. It exudes confidence, not arrogance.

3. It clearly and obviously nails every single job requirement at a glance.

But how can you be sure?

Try giving your resume to someone you know will give you strong feedback (hint: your mother is not one of them). Give them the sheet of requirements and ask them to go through your resume and mark off everything they can find on the list. Even better, pick someone who is not familiar with the industry, as they can help you find areas that you can make more accessible. When they have placed the right number of ticks (that you hoped for) beside each role requirement, you know you're ready for the next step.

4.8.   What to do if you know you don't meet all requirements?

You've just spent a lot of time capturing and tweaking all the things you've ever experienced and achieved (hopefully you were exhaustive). You've also spent a lot of time researching everything your prospective employer is looking for in that specific role. In order for you to get the job, these two things have to match. But what if they don't?

One mistake I see a lot of applicants making is simply not being honest with themselves: they tend to try and define a personal sales pitch that their "personal assets" cannot support. Not to say that you should not be aspirational, but you have to tie things you have done in the real world to your story in a supportive way.

If you find yourself unable to meet the requirements of the job you want, you still have options. Although this topic warrants an entire book on its own, I offer three indirect routes you can follow:

- **Take a long shot, and craft the best resume you can given your known limitations**—focus on meeting as many of the important requirements as possible, and emphasize other supporting strengths.

- **Find the side door**—internships, temp roles, or other support roles may allow you to transition into your desired role later.

- **Go build the right assets**—When all else fails, your best bet is to take a detour—go and build the experience and resume that will get you hired.

4.8.1.   Take a long shot, and craft the best resume you can within your known limitations.

So you've decided you want to take the long shot. Unless you're applying to somewhere like McKinsey (which limits how often you can reapply once rejected to one to two years), it certainly can't do you any harm. As a wise member of my family used to say about golf, "Research shows that 100 percent of the balls that didn't reach the hole, also didn't go in". So how should you go about it?

1. **Start by being very honest with yourself about where you fall short.** Which of the role requirements are you lacking evidence for? Note that you may feel you have the skill or competence, but lack evidence in your resume, in which case you have to make a really strong case for on-the-job learning.

2. **Determine how critical those requirements are to success within the role.** If you're applying to be a computer engineer, then a computer science degree is significantly more important than "the ability to work in teams". If you fall short in less critical areas, then you can bolster your evidence in areas in which you show strength.

3. **Some skill requirements are clear necessities, whereas others allow you more scope to differentiate yourself.** Typically the hardest requirement gaps to overcome involve role-related knowledge, since in all other categories there is at least some overlap and scope for fungibility.

4. **You need to at least try to address the unmet requirements by finding analogies or comparable activities** that can be used to make a case for the things you lack. For example one of the most important things consulting firms like McKinsey want to see is evidence of the ability to take a large ambiguous problem, independently structure it, and present coherent and well synthesized solutions.

5. **You can make up for a lack of consulting experience by translating activities in your other jobs into the framework of structured ambiguous problem solving.** A more common case could be demonstrating extensive experiential knowledge to make up for formal qualifications you may lack. Program or project management requirements could be addressed this way potentially.

6. **Convince the recruiter that other strengths you possess could distinguish you in the job at hand.** Job descriptions are typically minimalistic, and do not necessarily include other abilities that could be decisive in doing an excellent job. You need to make a compelling case for meeting as many of the minimums as possible, as well as bringing additional value to the table.

4.8.2. There is no shame in getting in through the side door.

If the direct route is blocked to you, there are indirect routes you should seriously consider. If you really have your heart set on a position, then swallow your pride, be prepared for a pay cut, and put aside notions of recruiters chasing you down and making special arrangements for you. If you're trying to climb a different ladder from the one you're on, you have to be prepared to start on the first rung. Here are a couple of indirect routes you can try:

- **Internships**—If you're young enough and lucky enough then you may be able to find an internship or leadership rotation program to participate in. You'll have to work for free (or for very little), but it will give you the ability to impress managers and recruiters who can make a case to bring you on full-time.

- **Temp roles**—A more likely avenue, if you're too old to qualify for an internship, is a temp role. Be prepared to prostrate yourself and take on potentially menial tasks that you may feel are beneath you. Remember the most important thing is to get your foot in the door. Once you're there, do everything you're asked exceptionally well, take on as much additional responsibility as possible, and rapidly make yourself indispensable to your team by demonstrating commitment, humility and the ability to build long-term relationships.

  This route often allows you to sidestep the onerous and arcane screening practices that companies hold dear and once you have people to "pound the table for you" internally, many of the requirements that initially prevented you from being considered can be set aside.

- **Support or ancillary roles**—Internal or lateral transfers within a company are almost always significantly easier than dealing with external hiring. Apply for a different role at the same company whose requirements you clearly exceed, even to the point of being potentially over-qualified, then do a knockout job. You will have influential supporters, exclusive internal knowledge of how the company works, and access to training materials and content that will assist you in learning the required skills.

Build a launch pad for yourself by very deliberately and actively developing both a network of strong supporters and a base of specialist experiential knowledge where possible. You should also actively court managers and mentors in the area you dream of working, who can assist you in planning a transfer when the time is right.

Critical to this strategy of entry through the side door, is to treat the role you're hired for as an important end in-and-of-itself, worthy of being taken seriously. Nobody likes to think of themselves as another person's stepping stone (even though that might be true), so if they even get a whiff of your intent they will be unlikely to hire you. You will only succeed in the transfer if you do an exceptional job in the one you're hired to do. Focus on that above all.

4.8.3. Take a detour—go get the experiences to build the required personal assets.

Lastly, and most indirectly, you may need to start your quest by investigating similar roles at lesser-known companies. Such companies tend to look more for generalist skills, have far less competition, and emphasize specific requirements less aggressively or have a lower bar for them.

This would give you an opportunity to gain the experience and build the skills you need, before applying again to your dream company at a later stage. Needless to say, before taking such a role you should do your homework:

- Will your job give you exposure to the exact skills and experiences listed in the requirements of your dream role? Can you influence your job scope or is there the potential to increase your responsibility to cover the dream role requirements?

- Are there similarities between the culture of your stepping-stone company and your dream company?

- Is your stepping-stone company known or admired by people in your dream company? Entrepreneurial exploits often tick this box, however working at a different big company with seemingly antithetical values or working styles would not. Choose wisely.

CHAPTER 5

5. Perfect your personal pitch by infusing your personal brand

S o now you have a detailed list of achievements that meet all of the job requirements. What next? Imagine that you and the CEO of your prospective company get into an elevator together, and enjoy an undisturbed five-minute ride to the top floor. You have a brief shot at making an impression, after which they have to want to learn more about you. An interview is not too dissimilar in reality, as your interviewer typically makes up their mind in the first five minutes.

How would you use those five minutes to convince someone that they should hear more? How would you want them to remember you?

> **OUTPUT - By the end of this Chapter, you will have:**
>
> 1. **Come up with a totally unique personal value proposition** that expresses your most compelling benefits.
>
> 2. **Combined the three facets of industry, company and personal value proposition** to tell a compelling story to potential recruiters why they should hire you.
>
> 3. **Created a personal sales pitch,** in the ideal medium, which highlights your perfect fit and unique selling points, and also adds color and character to the more fact-based resume.

5.1. Your benefits—the three most outstanding and valuable things about you.

I would divide most of the candidates I've seen over the years into three groups:

*   Those that waffle incessantly about their abilities despite either having no evidence of them, or worse, giving clear signals to the contrary.

*   Those that have no idea what their unique abilities and benefits are, and so consequently believe they have none.

*   Those that have connected their unique abilities and benefits to the facts of what they have achieved, and can talk about them with modest confidence.

Any idea which bucket you'd rather be in? The key to having the confidence in what you're selling is having the facts to back them up. I guarantee that the first time you try telling another person what you're good at, you will feel like the "Emperor with no clothes". There are two things you have to do to overcome this: (1) spend time building a solid link between the facts on your resume and each benefit you would like to sell; and (2) practice telling as many people as possible.

5.1.1. Step 1: Identify your three most important benefits to an employer.

This is harder than it seems, since you are constrained by your own perspective on the world. Try to write down what you think your most important abilities and traits are. But don't stop there. Talk to as many people as you feel comfortable, including close friends, peers you've worked with in the past, former managers, and mentors who have taken an active role in your development. Ask them to be really honest with you, and be ready to accept whatever feedback they give you with the intent of helping you know yourself and improve.

	Known to self	Not known to self
Known to others	Arena	Blind Spot
Not known to others	Façade	Unknown

Group all of these attributes according to the 2x2 above, known as your Johari window (source: Wikipedia).

By the end of this exercise you should aim to make the "arena" as large and as well-supported with facts as possible, select the best traits from the "façade" and bring them into the "arena" through your resume, and finally reduce your "blind spot" by really listening to the feedback you receive from those that care about you, and internalizing what they are saying.

After writing down as many benefits as you can, your last challenge is to group and prioritize them into just three potent and hard-hitting benefits that you can really sell about yourself.

5.1.2. Step 2: Support your top three benefits with facts from your resume.

Now take three colored pens/highlighters and assign a color to each benefit. Read through your resume, highlighting any evidence you have for each benefit in its respective color. If your benefits are reflective of your experience and achievements, then your page should be more or less fully colored in, and more or less evenly distributed across the three colors. If this is not the pattern you see, then either you have the wrong benefits, or you need to find some more evidence about what you're asserting. Again, having fact-based evidence for your benefits is the real way to go from delusional to confident.

5.1.3. Step 3: Practice saying it out loud.

When it comes time to describe to an interviewer what you're great at, you have to actually believe in what you're saying in order to be convincing, and that takes practice. Find a few people you trust, ask them to pretend they are interviewing you for this particular role, and start off by telling them the three reasons why you should be hired. It's going to feel strange, but the purpose is to get used to how your sales pitch sounds.

5.2. Putting it all together in a personal sales pitch.

Your application needs to flow seamlessly from your history, to your resume, to your story of why you want to work at that specific company. One tool intended to communicate this, which has become somewhat outdated of late, is the cover letter. Although typically barbarized today as a wordier version of the resume, the underlying raison d'être of the cover letter is to create a punchy account of the link between your features (in your resume) and your benefits.

Even if your prospective company doesn't require a cover letter from you, I highly recommend that you take the time to write one, since the content will form the cornerstone of any other format you may choose to convey your message in. Your cover letter is the first document in which you finally tie everything this book has covered so far into three succinct paragraphs:

Cover letter recipe: Three paragraphs, three Why's.

1.   Why that industry?

2.   Why that specific company and not "companies like this one"?

3.   Why do you fit perfectly into that role in that company?

5.2.1. Industry fit.

You've done all of your industry research, and developed some reasonable and informed opinions about why you want to work in that space. Use the first paragraph of your cover letter to describe how your passion, your interests and your experience contribute to a great industry match.

5.2.2. Company fit.

Recruiters and employees really dislike candidates who do not take a direct interest in their specific company. They will also make judgments about you based on both the range of companies you have worked for, as well as the range of companies to which you are currently applying (see Chapter 3 on "Why interviewers are like needy boyfriends/ girlfriends"). Make sure that anything you communicate to the company tells the same coherent story: tying together the company and culture research you did, with your experience, values and aspirations.

5.2.3. Role fit.

Finally, you want to use the last paragraph to outline the three benefits you identi-fied in the previous chapter, and how they directly impact the nature and require-ments of the role to which you're applying. Take the time to reinforce the benefits you assert by linking them to the facts in your resume, and in particular the impact you had in your past endeavors through those activities. Random assertions of your own aptitude are easily dismissed, but linking tangible impact you've achieved in the past to an ability or strength you bring increases your credibility.

5.2.4. Enhance your credibility—coherence and consistency.

Employers and recruiters that take an interest in you will typically do their home-work. Formal reference checks are one part of that, but simply Googling you will often get them pretty far. Once you have crafted the punchy pitch document above, make sure that all of your online and offline personas and platforms reflect the same story, including your Twitter account, any personal blogs you may have, and any other interesting query results that may reaffirm the points you've made.

5.3. Selecting a more creative medium for the message.

The output of this personal sales pitch can take many forms, the most traditional and simplest of which is the cover letter. However you may feel that your value is better expressed through a more creative medium:

- Any number of creative but non-traditional resume formats

- An Amazon product listing

- A Facebook profile page spoof

- A well-produced viral video embedded within a custom web site - http://googlepleasehire.me

These alternative forms can be very risky (less so for a designer than for a banker) as they require a lot of creativity, excellent execution, and originality. Copycats are easily uncovered, so don't simply rip off the ideas mentioned above. Even if done right, such alternative formats and stunts can only get you to the interview, where you will still be evaluated based on your story and demonstrated skills—although Matthew Epstein from googlepleashire.me fame got an interview at Google, he wasn't made an offer. This doesn't mean his pitch was a failure though! Because of the buzz he had generated, he ended up getting an equally exciting role at a start-up he loved, proving that once you figure out how to make a memorable pitch, other paths will open for you.

Once you have a clearer idea of which benefits you want to sell, **the right medium to convey these benefits and get noticed will often become more obvious** (see Chapter 6 on getting your resume into the right hands). Pick something that is relevant to the company and role you're applying for, rather than simply for the sake of the gimmick. If the medium in any way muddies or detracts from your core message, then you should keep simplifying until only the message remains.

CHAPTER 6

6. Signal vs. noise—get your resume into the right hands

T he most popular jobs typically have thousands of applicants a year. Recruiters are simply unable to read through that many resumes in such a short space of time and still give each one the attention it deserves. **What you need to do is to cut through the noise and grab the recruiter's attention**. Think very seriously about this. If you are just dropping your application through the one-way online form and hoping for the best, you're unlikely to get so much as a callback.

Now that your resume is short, punchy and formatted to draw the screener's eyes to the most important keywords, you're in as good a shape as you can be on paper. Unfortunately that isn't enough. You need someone in the company to take your resume, slap it down on their desk, and tell them to give you a call immediately. But how?

OUTPUT - By the end of this Chapter, you will have:

1. **Found potential referral entry points into your target company** through friends, friends-of-friends, or friends-of-friends-of-friends.

2. **Found a way to differentiate yourself through insight or content,** and found a way to get that content in front of someone that matters.

3. **Optimize your LinkedIn profile so you are easy to find,** and easy to notice in search results.

6.1. Get referred, any way you can.

Here's an inside tip you may not know—most companies reward their employees handsomely for successfully referring great new employees. That's right. Employees actually get paid to find and coach good talent. Not just that, but referred candidates typically have a separate application pile, with turnaround times of less than a week (versus months or years). Employees typically write a few paragraphs describing your relationship and commenting on your abilities, and these references are heavily weighed in the screening and hiring decision.

So why aren't you taking advantage of this glorious confluence of incentives?

1. **Search your networks** (LinkedIn is a great start) for people currently employed at your desired company.

2. **Reach out to them tactfully;** ask for advice, build a relationship, and convince them that you are worth a shot.

3. **Seed them with the content** for the reference they write about you by getting their feedback on your cover letter and resume—you want their words to echo your personal pitch.

Be humble and obliging. Employees do not lose face by sending in many applications for solid candidates who don't quite meet the requirements. They do however lose face if they submit candidates that come across as self-entitled, arrogant or pushy. Respect the fact that someone is taking a chance on you.

6.2. Getting noticed by senior people with power is a distant second.

If you can't find a peer or friend to refer you, then your next best option is to get noticed by a senior person with influence—someone to push the HR team to reach out to you.

A friend of mine used this approach to perfection in landing a role at a prominent venture capital company:

- He chose to write a Master's dissertation on a particular aspect of venture fund-raising that he was passionate about, and developed deep content expertise through original research.

- He turned his long thesis into a simple, punchy and attractive presentation, which he posted on Scribd and marketed to his network on Twitter and Quora (a question and answer platform).

- He actively engaged in questions and discussions about this specialized area on Quora using this new knowledge, to convey his new expertise, and referenced his published document each time.

- He paid close attention to the people engaging with his content, and when he noticed that a senior partner at a firm he admired posted a comment, he immediately engaged him and asked if they could meet for coffee.

How can you achieve the same kind of results without publishing a Master's dissertation?

1. **Start by identifying either a specialized piece of domain knowledge or a specific and unique skill** you possess (or would like to acquire) and one you believe a senior person at your prospective company would be highly interested.

2. **Turn that knowledge or skill into a tangible piece of content** that you can publish, seek feedback on, and iterate on until you start to gain traction.

3. **Fish where the fish are**—find out where the decision makers at your target firm are interacting online, and present your improved material to them (tactfully).

4. **Take your chance**—when the opportunity arises to engage with a target executive or influencer, make sure you jump on it. Be bold enough to ask for a chance to show your stuff. Use the short sales pitch you have developed through this book, and elaborate when asked. You will probably only get one chance, so make it count.

6.3. Turn your LinkedIn profile into low-hanging fruit for overworked recruiters and headhunters.

LinkedIn offers an amazing opportunity to be found by recruiters and head-hunters. As with anything though, getting your profile to stand out from the 200+ million other members requires some careful thinking. The people that you want to find you should be able to easily pick your profile out of the first page of search results for a limited set of keywords that match your skills and assets. Your job is to optimize your profile in order to be easily found and instantly noticed.

6.3.1. Keep your profile up-to-date, and add the color of your personal story.

You've made it through the long process of fine-tuning your past activities and achievements, and linking them to the most valuable aspects of your knowledge and abilities. Put that content to good use, ensuring that your punchy and impact-filled bullet points are described in each previous role you've held. Add a short synopsis of your cover letter to the "summary section", and ensure you have a clean headshot profile picture looking directly into the camera (studies show this greatly enhances trust).

6.3.2. Descriptive keywords are the first step to being found.

Find the broadest set of keywords from your resume and cover letter that describe you, and that also capture some of your unique abilities. Think of combinations of traits and keywords that others are less likely to have. Leaving your title as "consultant" will inevitably leave you drowned out amongst the millions of other plain-vanilla-consultants on the platform.

Brandon Trew

Google Product Manager ★ Product Area Privacy Lead ★ Former technology & operations strategy associate

San Francisco Bay Area | Internet

Current	**Product Manager** at **Google**
Past	Strategy Associate at Google
	Consultant at Royal Bafokeng Administration
	Strategic Executive at Craft-ED (UK) Limited
	Founder and director at Selador Capital
	Business Analyst at McKinsey & Company
	see less ▴
Education	University of Oxford - Said Business School
	University of Cape Town

Instead, **take the 120-character opportunity to add a wider range of keywords** that summarize more of your key benefits. Not only are you more likely to surface in search results, but when you do, your profile will convey more to the recruiter in a glance, and make it more likely that they click on your name to find out more. Apply this same keyword thinking to all job titles, job descriptions and interests. The more words and phrases that match the recruiters' queries, the more you'll be found. Be careful not to overdo it. Many people are put off by profiles that are too good. Do enough to be found, but be wary of appearing too focused on networking and schmoozing.

6.3.3. Additional search optimization tweaks to get you to the top of the results.

- **Ensure you switch your default profile URL** (web address) for a "vanity" URL, which surfaces better both within LinkedIn and more broadly in Google and other search engine results:

  🔲 www.linkedin.com/in/brandontrew/

- **Ask peers and managers you have worked with in previous roles to write you a recommendation.** Be sure to contact your reviewers beforehand to discuss the talking points from your cover letter. This will ensure that your story and your peer feedback really hang together coherently.

- **Grow your network.** The more connections you have, the more important LinkedIn thinks you are, and the higher you'll rank in the search results.

CHAPTER 7

7. In conclusion: To get hired, know yourself, know the role, sell the perfect fit

My goal with this book is to get you past the interview gatekeeper and into the interview for your dream role. If you've completed all of the exercises in this book, you should have all the underpinnings of a successful application:

- **A real understanding** of the most valuable things about you, and why organizations should be interested in hiring you.

- **A great looking resume** that recruiters can easily pick out of a large stack at a glance.

- **A punchy cover letter** that offers a true synthesis of your value and describes why you're a perfect fit for the company and role.

- **The ideal channel** for getting your resume into the hands of someone who matters, and who can invite you to an interview.

As per my challenge to you in Chapter 1, take a second to compare what you have now, to what you started with. I'd love to hear any feedback about how you feel after this process, how your applications went, and how I could make this book better (@brandontrew).

A couple of things should be clear at this point about what you need to do:

- **Hyper-tailored**—Your recruiters are looking for something really specific for each role, so make sure you meet as many of both the explicit and implicit job requirements as possible.

- **Know yourself**—Be really, painfully honest about what you're great at, and why someone should want to hire you. Practice saying it out loud, and make sure you feel comfortable and confident with what you're selling.

- **Sell yourself**—You have to take a long hard look at yourself, figure out how best to package yourself and your talents, and then maximize your chance of being found amidst a very large and competitive market.

- **You have to want it**—Make no mistake; recruiters and interviewers are not interested in people who are lukewarm. They are not interested in candidates that feel entitled, or who believe that they are too good for a company or position. To be taken seriously, you need to humble yourself and really commit to applying for each job.

- **Be modestly confident**—Interviewers respond best to confidence inspired by evidence and impact. Hopefully this preparation has given you the assets to feel like you are prepared, capable, and ready.

That's it, you're ready! Congratulations on making it through the application preparation process. Hopefully you feel considerably better prepared and equipped to go after the role you most desire, and with a little luck you will soon be invited in for an interview.

Don't rest on your laurels at this stage. Be aware that you still have an enormous amount of work to do sharpening your live interview skills and putting some of that fantastic research you've just completed to good use.

If you'd like more information about how to get through the interview, please check out my upcoming book (due later in 2013) in the Kindle Store—**"The inside guide to Case Interviews: and how to get out of the blender".** Or check in at inside-guides.com for updates.

I'd like to wish you the best of luck with your future endeavors and applications. Please keep the feedback coming.

About the Author

I am:

- **Passionate about and interested in building great products** and platforms that take us closer to the Singularity.

- **A failed-and-reborn entrepreneur,** tech geek, aspirant photographer and futurist daydreamer.

- **An author,** having published a book "Stand out, fit in, get hired.", and an 8-part video training series on Excel Modeling Perfection (see http://brandontrew.com for details).

- **A proven execution specialist,** having dreamed up, project-managed and launched numerous complex, cross-functional and high-impact projects and products at Google and elsewhere.

- **A technology strategist,** experienced in local shopping, digital offers and coupons, display ads, digital media and online privacy strategy.

- **A recovering consultant,** experienced in global supply chain, route-to-market, organizational design and national education system turn-around strategy.

- **A proud South African.**

Contact me at: @brandontrew, or at http://brandontrew.com

Printed in Great Britain
by Amazon